RAINTREE BIOGRAPHIES

Benjamin Franklin

Janet Riehecky

RAINTREE STECK-VAUGHN PUBLISHERS

A Harcourt Company

Austin   New York
www.raintreesteckvaughn.com

Published by Raintree Steck-Vaughn Publishers, an imprint of Steck-Vaughn Company.

Project Editors: Sean Dolan, Leigh Ann Cobb, Gianna Williams
Production Manager: Richard Johnson
Designed by Ian Winton

Planned and produced by Discovery Books

Library of Congress Cataloging-in-Publication Data
Available upon request.

ISBN 0-7398-5675-8

Printed and bound in China.
1 2 3 4 5 6 7 8 9 0 MID 07 06 05 04 03 02

Acknowledgments
The publishers would like to thank the following for permission to reproduce their pictures:
Cover, pp.4 & 5 Peter Newark's American Pictures; pp.6, 7 & 8 Mary Evans Picture Library; pp.9, 10, 11 & 12 Peter
Newark's American Pictures; 13 Mary Evans Picture Library; pp.14, 15, 16, 17, 18, 19 & 20 Peter Newark's American
Pictures; p.21 Mary Evans Picture Library; pp.22 & 23 Peter Newark's American Pictures; p.24 Grainger Collection; p.25
Corbis; p.26 Bridgeman Art Library; pp.27 & 28 Corbis; p.29 Peter Newark's American Pictures.

CONTENTS

Helping His Country

In September 1776, the American colonies needed help to win their independence from Britain. They sent a 70-year-old man, Benjamin Franklin, to France to ask for help. Franklin was popular and well-respected in France.

Benjamin Franklin became famous throughout the world for his scientific, literary, and diplomatic accomplishments.

It took him a year to negotiate a treaty of alliance with France. France recognized the United States as an independent nation, declared war on Britain, and promised to supply the United States with money, equipment, a powerful navy, and thousands of troops. Without that aid, it is unlikely the U.S. would have won the war.

FLYING A KITE

There is a famous story about how Franklin proved lightning was a form of electricity. Franklin attached a metal wire to the top of a kite and a key to the string. When lightning hit the wire, it flowed down to the key, just like electricity. Franklin himself never mentioned the story, and historians are not sure it ever really happened.

Benjamin Franklin was not just a skilled diplomat: he was a great philosopher, writer, publisher, inventor, scientist, philanthropist, and businessman. Most importantly, he helped the United States become a nation.

CHILDHOOD IN BOSTON

Benjamin Franklin was born on January 17, 1706, in Boston, Massachusetts. His father, Josiah, was a soap and candle maker who had left England so he could practice his religion, Presbyterianism, without fear of persecution. He had settled in Massachusetts, one of the 13 British colonies in America. Josiah had 17 children. Ben was the fifteenth child and the youngest son. Franklin's mother, Abiah, was Josiah's second wife.

Ben could read by the age of 4. He learned easily. His father decided to send him to grammar school when he was 8. Josiah thought Ben might become a minister. In school Ben was good at reading and writing, but he had trouble with math. After two years Josiah found he couldn't afford to keep Ben in school. He also thought Ben wasn't religious enough to be a minister, so Ben had to learn a trade.

This large frame house, located in Boston, is the birthplace of Benjamin Franklin.

For two years his father taught him about the soap and candle-making business, but Ben didn't really like it. He wanted to become a sailor, but his father had already lost one of his sons to the sea. Josiah thought it would be better for Ben to be apprenticed to another brother, James, a printer.

In the early 1700s, making soap or candles was hard work. Some of Ben's duties included filling the molds for candles, manning the shop, and running errands.

APPRENTICES

In the 18th century, most children did not go to school. By the age of 12, many were apprenticed. The children went to live with their master, who fed, clothed, and housed them. The master taught them a skill, such as shoemaking or blacksmithing. In return, the child worked without pay until the age of 21.

A PRINTER AND A WRITER

Ben was 12 when he went to live with James. Ben liked the printing business and became very good at the trade. But James beat him and made him work very hard.

Ben lived in Boston until he was 17. During the 18th century, Boston harbor was one of the busiest ports in North America.

Soon, Ben started writing his own works. When he was 15, his brother began publishing a newspaper called the *New England Courant*. Ben made up a character called Silence Dogood, an older woman who poked fun at people who took themselves too seriously. Ben pretended that someone slipped her letters under the door of the printing office.

James printed 13 letters from Silence Dogood. Everyone liked them, but James was angry when he found out it was Ben who had written them.

In 1723, James printed a letter in his newspaper that criticized local politicians for not doing enough to stop piracy at sea. This was not the first time he had disagreed with the authorities in print, and he was sent to jail. When he was released, he was forbidden to publish the newspaper, so he put it in Ben's name. To do this, he had to say Ben was no longer an apprentice, but he made Ben sign secret papers saying he was still under James's control. Ben decided to leave. He knew his brother couldn't show the papers to anyone. Still, James made sure that Ben did not get any printing work in Boston.

Benjamin Franklin as a young man. Franklin had barely enough money to buy bread after he ran away from Boston.

A SUCCESSFUL PUBLISHER

Ben, now 17, went to New York City to look for work. A printer there told him there might be work in Philadelphia. Ben took a boat to Pennsylvania and then walked 50 miles to Philadelphia. He arrived tired, hungry, and broke, but he found a job with a printer named Samuel Keimer.

When Ben's brother-in-law, Robert Holmes, found out that Ben was in Philadelphia, he wrote to him, asking him to come back to Boston. Ben wrote back, saying that he was staying in Philadelphia. When the letter arrived, Holmes showed it to the governor of Pennsylvania, who happened to be there.

Franklin in his printing shop. One of his first money-making ventures was the printing of the Pennsylvania Gazette, *considered one of the finest colonial newspapers.*

The governor was impressed with Franklin's writing and offered to set him up in his own shop in London, England, promising to provide letters of introduction and money. Franklin sailed to London, but the letters never arrived. Instead, he got a job with a printer and worked there for two years.

In 1726, Franklin returned to Philadelphia and worked for Samuel Keimer, but eventually he opened his own printing shop. In 1729, he began publishing a newspaper, the *Pennsylvania Gazette*. In 1730, he married Deborah Read, the daughter of the family he had stayed with when he first arrived in Philadelphia.

Poor Richard, 1733.
AN
Almanack
For the Year of Christ
1733,
Being the First after LEAP YEAR:

	Years
And makes since the Creation	
By the Account of the Eastern Greeks	7241
By the Latin Church, when O ent. ♈	6932
By the Computation of W.W.	5742
By the Roman Chronology	5682
By the Jewish Rabbies	5494

Wherein is contained
The Lunations, Eclipses, Judgment of the Weather, Spring Tides, Planets Motions & mutual Aspects, Sun and Moon's Rising and Setting, Length of Days, Time of High Water, Fairs, Courts, and observable Days
Fitted to the Latitude of Forty Degrees and a Meridien of Five Hours West from London, but may without sensible Error serve all the adjacent Places, even from Newfoundland to South-Carolina.
By RICHARD SAUNDERS, Philom.
PHILADELPHIA:
Printed and sold by B. FRANKLIN, at the New Printing-Office near the Market.

POOR RICHARD'S ALMANACK

Almanacs (spelt "almanacks" in Franklin's day) are calendars that include weather forecasts and interesting facts. In 1732, Franklin began publishing *Poor Richard's Almanack*. It became the most popular almanac in America. People still quote its sayings, such as "Early to bed and early to rise, makes a man healthy, wealthy, and wise." Franklin published one a year for 25 years.

SCIENTIST AND INVENTOR

Franklin worked very hard in his printing shop. By 1748, his business was worth £2,000 (a high court judge of the time made around £200 a year). He had made enough money to retire. He began to turn his hand to scientific experiments.

Scientists in Franklin's day were very interested in electricity. Franklin was the first person to prove that lightning is electricity. He invented the lightning rod, a metal bar that is attached to the top of a house. Lightning is drawn to it and passes through it harmlessly. Before this, when lightning struck a house, it usually set the house on fire.

By the age of 42, Franklin had made enough money to retire.

In 1742, most people used fireplaces to heat their homes. Franklin saw that most of the heat went up the chimney. He invented an iron stove. The sides of the stove helped send heat out into the room.

THE ARMONICA

Franklin invented a musical instrument, the armonica. It had 37 glass bowls that were rotated through water. Rubbing the wet rims produced a clear, bell-like tone. Both Mozart and Beethoven composed music for the armonica, but the instrument was too fragile to be practical.

Franklin invented many practical objects, including bifocal glasses to help himself read. He also invented the odometer, a device to measure how many miles something has traveled, a mechanical arm to reach into high places, and the rocking chair. He never took out a patent on any of his inventions, because he wanted everyone to benefit from them. Franklin's discoveries were printed in pamphlets that were read all over the 13 colonies and Europe.

Franklin had a natural curiosity about how things work and how to make them work better.

FRANKLIN THE PHILOSOPHER

In 1727, while still working as a printer, Franklin started a club where men met to discuss ideas and learn together. He called it the Junto, Spanish for "together." It was also called the "Leather Apron Club," because its members were all craftsmen who usually wore leather aprons while they worked.

The Junto met each Friday evening for about 30 years. The men in the Junto often borrowed books from each other.

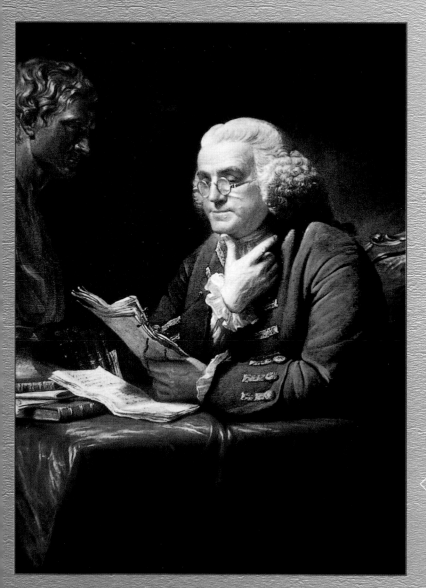

Franklin suggested that all the books be kept in a central location where they could be organized. People could pay a small fee for the privilege of checking books out. The money could be used to buy more books. This was the first subscription library in America. Soon many communities throughout the colonies started one of their own.

Franklin in his study. The members of the Junto read essays together and discussed ideas about philosophy, science, or business.

The 13 Virtues

Franklin had a list of 13 virtues, and every day wrote down how he had performed in each of them:

1. Temperance—Eat not to dullness; drink not to elevation.
2. Silence—Speak not but what may benefit others or yourself; avoid trifling conversation.
3. Order—Let all your things have their places; let each part of your business have its time.
4. Resolution—Resolve to perform what you ought; perform without fail what you resolve.
5. Frugality—Make no expense but to do good to others or yourself; i.e. waste nothing.
6. Industry—Lose no time; be always employ'd in something useful; cut off all unnecessary actions.
7. Sincerity—Use no hurtful deceit; think innocently and justly, and, if you speak, speak accordingly.
8. Justice—Wrong none by doing injuries, or omitting the benefits that are your duty.
9. Moderation—Avoid extreme; forbear resenting injuries so much as you think they deserve.
10. Cleanliness—Tolerate no uncleanliness in body, clothes, or habitation.
11. Tranquility—Be not disturbed at trifles, or at accidents common or unavoidable.
12. Chastity—Rarely use venery [sexual relations] but for health or offspring, never to dullness, weakness, or the injury of your own or another's peace of reputation.
13. Humility—Imitate Jesus and Socrates.

In 1751, Franklin helped organize the Academy for the Education of Youth in Philadelphia. Eventually this school became the University of Pennsylvania. The Academy was different from most other colleges, which often taught only the classics and religious subjects. It also offered modern languages, history, science, and agriculture.

A page from "Articles of Belief and Acts of Religion," Franklin's religious creed, written in 1728.

PUBLIC SERVANT AND DIPLOMAT

Discussing ideas of how to improve himself led Franklin to think about how to improve his community. In 1736, Franklin formed a volunteer fire department in Philadelphia. Over the next several years he organized many more projects, such as having the streets paved, putting up street lights, opening an orphanage, and organizing a city police force.

In 1736, Franklin was elected to his first public office, clerk of the Pennsylvania legislature. This was an important position in which he was record keeper for the assembly. In 1748, he was elected as a member of the legislature. Rarely giving speeches, he worked behind the scenes to get things done. He was especially skilled at getting people who disagreed about something to compromise.

Franklin's buggy is stopped on the Boston Post Road in 1763.

Franklin's Plan of Union was adopted unanimously by the Albany Congress. The mission of the Plan of Union was that colonies be represented in the British Parliament. The British Parliament rejected the plan.

One of the most important positions Franklin held was postmaster for the colonies. As postmaster, he made many improvements to the mail service, such as hiring more couriers and requiring them to ride both day and night. He also found other speedy methods to get mail to its destination in a shorter amount of time In 1754, the Pennsylvania legislature asked him to travel north to the Albany Congress, where he tried to negotiate a peace treaty with the Indians.

IDEAS OF INDEPENDENCE

It was during the Albany Congress that Franklin decided the colonies should unite. "It would be a strange thing if six nations of [Indians] should be capable of forming a scheme for such a union... and yet that a like union should be impractical for ten or a dozen English colonies to whom it is more necessary."

FRANKLIN IN ENGLAND

From 1757 to 1759 and from 1764 to 1775, several colonies asked Franklin to represent them in London. Franklin tried to persuade the British government to be more fair in their taxes and to allow Americans to have a voice in the British Parliament. One tax in particular, brought under the Stamp Act, caused problems. Under the Act a tax was charged on all documents, such as newspapers, diplomas, and licenses. Franklin argued against it, but Parliament passed it anyway.

The colonists were very angry. They were upset about the tax, but even more about not having any representation in the Parliament that imposed the tax. They felt they had the right to elect the people who governed them. Franklin helped in persuading Parliament to repeal the Stamp Act, but he couldn't get them to agree to allow the colonies to elect representatives to Parliament.

Franklin (standing) defends America's rights to Parliament. His dignity in the Stamp Act debate won him prestige back home.

Even though Franklin was separated from his wife, Deborah (shown here), during his diplomatic missions, he loved her and credited her for much of his success.

The relationship between the colonies and Britain grew worse. Franklin felt he could no longer do any good in London. In 1775, Franklin learned that his wife, Deborah, who had stayed in America, had died of a stroke. He had not seen her for ten years. Shortly after that, he returned home.

THE THOMAS HUTCHISON LETTERS

Between 1767 and 1769, the governor of Massachusetts, Thomas Hutchison, wrote letters to England asking that the liberties of colonists be restricted. Franklin got hold of the letters and sent them to the Speaker of the Massachusetts House of Representatives. They soon became public, and Franklin was summoned before the British Parliament. After this, Franklin wrote many articles explaining American grievances. In 1773, he published *Rules by Which a Great Empire May Be Reduced to a Small One*.

Declaring Independence

On May 6, 1775, one day after he arrived back in America, 69-year-old Franklin was elected a delegate to the Second Continental Congress, a meeting of representatives from the 13 colonies.

Deserted by His Son

Franklin's son, William (right), became the Royal Governor of New Jersey and stayed loyal to England during the revolution. Franklin said, "Indeed nothing has ever hurt me so much and affected me with such keen sensations, as to find myself deserted in my old age by my only son; and not only deserted, but to find him taking up arms against me, in a cause wherein my good fame, fortune, and life were all at stake."

The colonies were on the verge of war with Britain. Franklin had already decided that independence was the only solution to their problems. He tried to get the other members of Congress to see this. He also worked to help set up a new government.

This draft of the Declaration of Independence shows the changes made by Franklin and John Adams.

He designed a paper currency, worked as postmaster general, and met with General George Washington to plan a strategy for the army. He arranged to purchase supplies, such as ammunition. Franklin also helped write the Declaration of Independence, which was approved on the 4th of July, 1776.

The original draft of the Declaration of Independence was written by Thomas Jefferson. But Franklin made some suggestions to make the wording simpler. For example, Jefferson wrote, "We hold these truths to be sacred and undeniable." Franklin suggested, "We hold these truths to be self-evident."

Words of Wisdom

At the signing of the Declaration, Franklin urged everyone to pull together saying, "Gentlemen, we must now hang together, or we shall most assuredly hang separately."

21

HELPING HIS COUNTRY IN FRANCE

After war was declared, Congress needed Franklin's diplomatic skills again. In September 1776, they sent him to France. France was a friendly country to the American revolutionaries. Franklin was very popular there. The French had read *Poor Richard's Almanack* and knew of his scientific experiments. Pictures of him were put on rings, buttons, plates, statues, and many other things. Ladies even wore their hair in a style resembling the fur hat he always wore.

Franklin first wore his fur hat to cover a skin disease, but the French thought it showed how humble he was.

There he was able to arrange for French aid and eventually French recognition of the United States as an independent nation.

Franklin in Paris

"Such a person was made to excite the curiosity of Paris. The people clustered around as he passed and asked, 'Who is this old peasant who has such a noble air?'"

Description of Franklin in Paris, **by Hilliard d'Auberteuil**

WORRYING THE BRITISH

British spies not only worried about Franklin's skills as a diplomat, but also as a scientist. One claimed that Franklin was assembling huge mirrors that would reflect the sun and burn up the British fleet. Another said he planned to send a jolt of electricity to Britain through a chain strung across the English Channel.

Many young men offered to help Franklin by joining the American forces. Among them was a Scotsman named John Paul Jones. He was a sea captain who became a naval hero. He named his ship, the *Bonhomme* (French for "good man") *Richard*, after Franklin's *Poor Richard's Almanack*. Franklin also sent two very able officers to America: Marie Joseph, the Marquis de Lafayette, and Friedrich Wilhelm, Baron von Steuben, both of whom became important aides to General Washington.

Franklin inspired many French fashions, including wearing hats with lightning conductors attached to them.

THE TREATY OF PARIS

After the British general Lord Cornwallis surrendered to the Americans in 1781, Franklin, John Adams, and John Jay negotiated the treaty with Britain that would end the war. It was signed September 3, 1783.

This portrait of the signing of the Treaty of Paris was left unfinished because the British refused to sit for the painting. Franklin is seated in the center.

In the Treaty of Paris, Britain agreed to acknowledge the full and complete independence of the United States of America. The boundaries of the U.S. were agreed upon, including all the land south of the Great Lakes and east of the Mississippi River, some of which had been claimed by Canada. Americans were also given the right to fish off the banks of Newfoundland and of navigation and commerce on the Mississippi River.

Franklin's long experience dealing with the governments of France and Spain enabled him to set the agenda. He worked out a list of essential and negotiable terms and got Britain to agree to them.

A Public Servant

Franklin believed that people in public office should not be paid for their work. "The pleasure of doing good and serving their Country and the respect such conduct entitles them to, are sufficient motives with some minds to give up a great portion of their time to the Public... ."

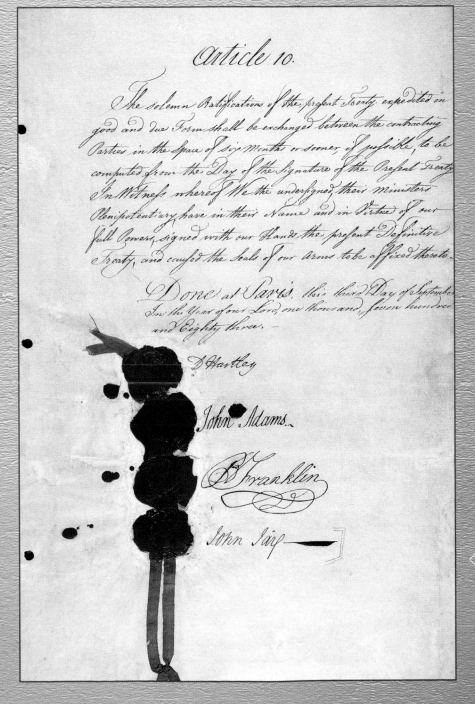

Although he asked to return to the United States, Franklin was kept in Paris until 1785 as a representative of Congress, making agreements between the United States and other nations. Franklin said that his time as a diplomat taught him that there was no such thing as a good war or a bad peace.

The American delegation used sealing wax to mark their signatures on the Treaty of Paris.

APPROVING THE CONSTITUTION

Franklin returned to the U.S. in 1785, intending to live out his final years in retirement. But his country called on him again. First he was elected to a seat on the Pennsylvania Executive Committee. Then, in 1787, he was asked to serve as one of the 55 delegates to the Constitutional Convention meeting in Philadelphia.

At the signing of the Constitution, Franklin suffered from arthritis and had to be carried into the courthouse.

A Prayer

Though Franklin had never been much of a churchgoer, he requested that the Convention open with a prayer. He said, "If a sparrow cannot fall to the ground without His notice, is it probable that an empire can rise without His aid?"

During the war, differences between the colonies had been put aside. Now that the war was over, there were many arguments over such things as borders between states and how much power should be given to the federal government.

Franklin spoke very little at the Convention. Sometimes when discussions grew tense, he lightened the atmosphere with a joke. His most important speech came after they had put together the Constitution. He was too weak to read it himself, but another delegate read it. Franklin asked the delegates to support the whole Constitution even if it wasn't perfect, so that the nation might be united.

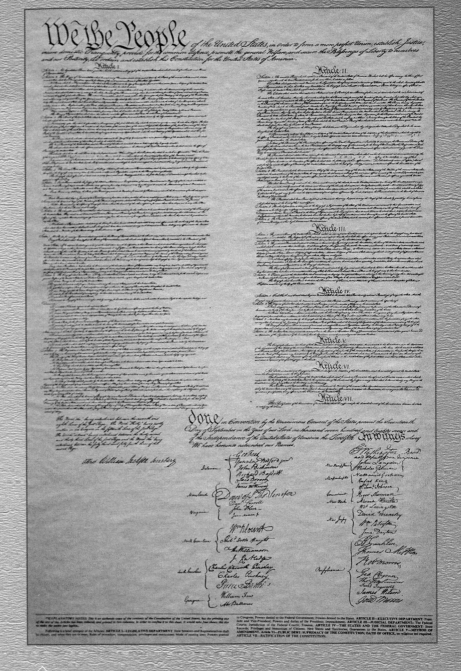

The U.S. Constitution was the first attempt to define in written form the rights and powers of the government and the people.

Ben Franklin lived two more years after the Convention. During his last year, he was so ill he did not leave his room. He was in constant pain, but refused to take opium to relieve it, so his mind could stay clear. He loved visitors, especially his grandchildren. He died on April 17, 1790.

THE LEGACY OF BEN FRANKLIN

Over 20,000 people followed the funeral procession of Ben Franklin. Flags were flown at half-mast and the House of Representatives went into mourning for a month.

More than two centuries after his death, people recognize and respect his great contributions. His early suffering at the hands of his brother James had given him a life-long love of freedom. As an author, he entertained and educated. As a scientist, he added to our knowledge of how things work.

A monument to Franklin stands outside Pennsylvania Hospital, which he helped to found in 1751. It is the oldest hospital in the United States.

ABOLISHING SLAVERY

Though Franklin had once owned slaves, by the 1780s he was convinced that slavery was inherently evil and had to be completely abolished. In 1787, he became president of the Society for Promoting the Abolition of Slavery and the Relief of Negroes Unlawfully Held in Bondage.

Epitaph written 1728.

The Body of
B Franklin Printer;
(Like the Cover of an old Book
Its Contents torn out
And stript of its Lettering & Gilding)
Lies here, Food for Worms.
But the Work shall not be lost;
For it will, (as he believ'd) appear once more,
In a new and more elegant Edition
Revised and corrected,
By the Author.

If Life's compared to a Feast,
Near Fourscore Years I've been a Guest;
I've been regaled with the best,
And feel quite satisfy'd.
'Tis time that I retire to Rest;
Landlord, I thank ye!—Friends, Good Night.

April 22. 1784 —

Franklin wrote his own epitaph when he was 22. He is buried in Christ Church Burial Grounds in Philadelphia. It reads:
The Body of B. Franklin Printer;
(Like the cover of an old book,
It's contents torn out,
And stript of its Lettering and Gilding)
Lies here, Food for Worms.
But the Work shall not be lost:
For it will (as he beliv'd) appear once more,
In a new and more elegant Edition Revised and corrected,
By the Author.

Many of the words we use today to talk about electricity were first invented by Ben Franklin. These include battery, charge, electrician, and more. His inventions helped improve people's lives. His ideas for community services made towns and cities safer and life easier. As a statesman, he helped the United States become a nation.

TIMELINE

January 17, 1706–Benjamin Franklin is born in Boston, Massachusetts.

1714–Attends school.

1716–Works in his father's shop.

1718–Becomes apprenticed to his brother James, a printer.

1722–Silence Dogood's letters published.

September 25, 1723–Franklin runs away from Boston; eventually settles in Philadelphia.

1724–Sails to London.

1726–Returns to Philadelphia.

1727–Starts the Junto or Leather Apron Club.

1728–Opens his own printing shop.

1729–Begins publishing his own newspaper, the *Pennsylvania Gazette*.

1730–Marries Deborah Read; son William is born.

1731–Sets up the first subscription library in America.

1732–Publishes the first edition of *Poor Richard's Almanack*; Oct. 20 son Francis is born.

1736–Francis Franklin dies from smallpox; Franklin elected clerk of the Pennsylvania Legislature; starts the Union Fire Company of Philadelphia.

1737–Appointed as postmaster of Philadelphia.

1742–Invents the Franklin stove.

August 31, 1743–daughter Sarah (Sally) is born.

1748–Retires from the printing business.

1752–His experiments show that lightning is a form of electricity.

1753–Appointed Postmaster for all the American colonies.

1757–Represents Pennsylvania legislature in London.

1762–Returns to Philadelphia.

1764–1775–Represents all the American colonies in London.

1772–Elected to the French Academy of Science.

December 1774–Deborah Franklin dies.

May 1775–return to Philadelphia; elected to the Second Continental Congress.

1776–Assists in writing the Declaration of Independence; he is one of the original signers.

1776–1785–U.S. ambassador to France.

1783–Helps write the Treaty of Paris ending the Revolutionary War.

1785–Returns to Philadelphia; elected president of Pennsylvania Assembly; elected member of the Constitutional Convention.

1787–Signs the Constitution of the United States.

April 17, 1790–Benjamin Franklin dies at the age of 84.

GLOSSARY

Acknowledge (ak-NOL-ij) To take official notice of.

Ambassador (am-BASS-uh-dur) A person sent to a foreign country to represent the interests of his/her homeland.

Colony (KOL-uh-nee) A settlement founded in a different country.

Compromise (KOM-pruh-mize) To resolve an argument by each side giving up something.

Conveniences (kuhn-VEEN-yences) Something that provides personal comfort or ease.

Delegate (DEL-uh-guht) A person who represents a group of people.

Diplomat (DIP-luh-mat) A person appointed by the government to work with the government of a foreign nation.

Negotiate (ni-GOH-shee-ate) To talk over an issue and come to an agreement.

Orphanage (OR-fuh-nij) A home for children whose parents have died.

Patent (PAT-uhnt) An official document that allows the inventor of a device to be the only one allowed to make or sell it.

Philanthropist (ful-LAN-thruh-pist) Someone who helps other people.

Philosophical (fil-uh-SOF-uh-kuhl) Having to do with studying the meaning of life.

Repeal (ri-PEEL) To set aside or take back.

Rotate (ROH-tate) To move in a circle around a central point.

Subscription (suhb-SKRIP-shuhn) An agreement to pay to receive something over a period of time.

Successor (suhk-SESS-ur) A person who takes over after another leaves a job or position.

FURTHER READING AND INFORMATION

Books to Read

Adler, David A. *Benjamin Franklin: Printer, Inventor, Statesman*. New York: Holiday House, 1992.

Lee, Tanja. *Benjamin Franklin (People Who Made History)*. San Diego, CA: Greenhaven Press, 2001.

Quackenbush, Robert. *Benjamin Franklin and His Friends*. New York: Pippin Press, 1991.

Rudy, Lisa Jo. *The Ben Franklin Book of Easy and Incredible Experiments*. New York: John Wiley & Sons, 1995.

Stine, Megan. *Ben Franklin Beware*. New York: Sundance Publishing, 1993.

Videos

Biography: Benjamin Franklin—Citizen of the World. A&E Biography, 1995.

Ben & Me. Walt Disney Home Video, 1998.

INDEX